STEM

Lasers

Measuring Length

Lisa M. Sill, M.A.

Publishing Credits

Rachelle Cracchiolo, M.S.Ed., *Publisher*
Conni Medina, M.A.Ed., *Managing Editor*
Dona Herweck Rice, *Series Developer*
Emily R. Smith, M.A.Ed., *Series Developer*
Diana Kenney, M.A.Ed., NBCT, *Content Director*
June Kikuchi, *Content Director*
Stacy Monsman, M.A., *Editor*
Michelle Jovin, M.A., *Assistant Editor*
Fabiola Sepulveda, *Graphic Designer*

Image Credits: pp.4, 20 (left), 21, 26 courtesy of NASA; p.18 Bernard Annebicque/Sygma/Sygma via Getty Images; p.19 Raphael Gaillarde/Gamma-Rapho via Getty Images; p.24 MTS Photo/Shutterstock; p.5 Toshifumi Kitamura/AFP/Getty Images; all other images from iStock and/or Shutterstock.

Library of Congress Cataloging-in-Publication Data

Names: Sill, Lisa M., author.
Title: STEM. Lasers / Lisa M. Sill.
Other titles: Lasers
Description: Huntington Beach, CA : Teacher Created Materials, [2018] | Includes index. | Audience: Grades K to 3. |
Identifiers: LCCN 2017049141 (print) | LCCN 2017059522 (ebook) | ISBN 9781425859435 (eBook) | ISBN 9781425857530 (pbk.)
Subjects: LCSH: Lasers--Juvenile literature.
Classification: LCC TA1682 (ebook) | LCC TA1682 .S55 2018 (print) | DDC 621.36/6--dc23
LC record available at https://lccn.loc.gov/2017049141

Teacher Created Materials
5301 Oceanus Drive
Huntington Beach, CA 92649-1030
http://www.tcmpub.com

ISBN 978-1-4258-5753-0

Printed by : 465482
Printed In : Malaysia / PO#15313

Table of Contents

What Are Lasers?

A laser is a device that makes a **beam** of light. It is a special form of light. It is not like sunlight. It is not like a flashlight, either. A laser is much more amazing!

The light from lasers can be used in many special ways. Lasers help people every day.

A scientist shines a laser up to the sky.

A scientist uses a laser in a lab.

Bright Lights

Lasers make very bright lights. In fact, they are the brightest **source** of light on Earth. The light from a laser can be up to one million times brighter than the light from a light bulb! This strong light can hurt people's eyes. But there are ways people can stay safe. The best way is to wear special glasses that block the bright light. They help protect people's vision.

A man wears special goggles to protect his eyes from laser light.

Light moves in waves. Light waves look like the waves in an ocean. But these waves will not get anyone wet. In fact, the human eye cannot even see them!

Light waves also move like a roller coaster. They go up and down over and over again. The distance between light waves is called the wavelength. Only certain wavelengths can be seen by the human eye.

ocean waves

This roller coaster has the same shape as light waves.

White Light vs. Laser Light

Light from the sun is called white light. White light is not really white. In fact, it is made up of seven different colors. White light is made up of red, orange, yellow, green, blue, indigo, and violet. These are all the colors of a rainbow.

Each color in white light has its own wavelength. They move at different speeds. This causes white light to **scatter**. Flashlights have white light beams.

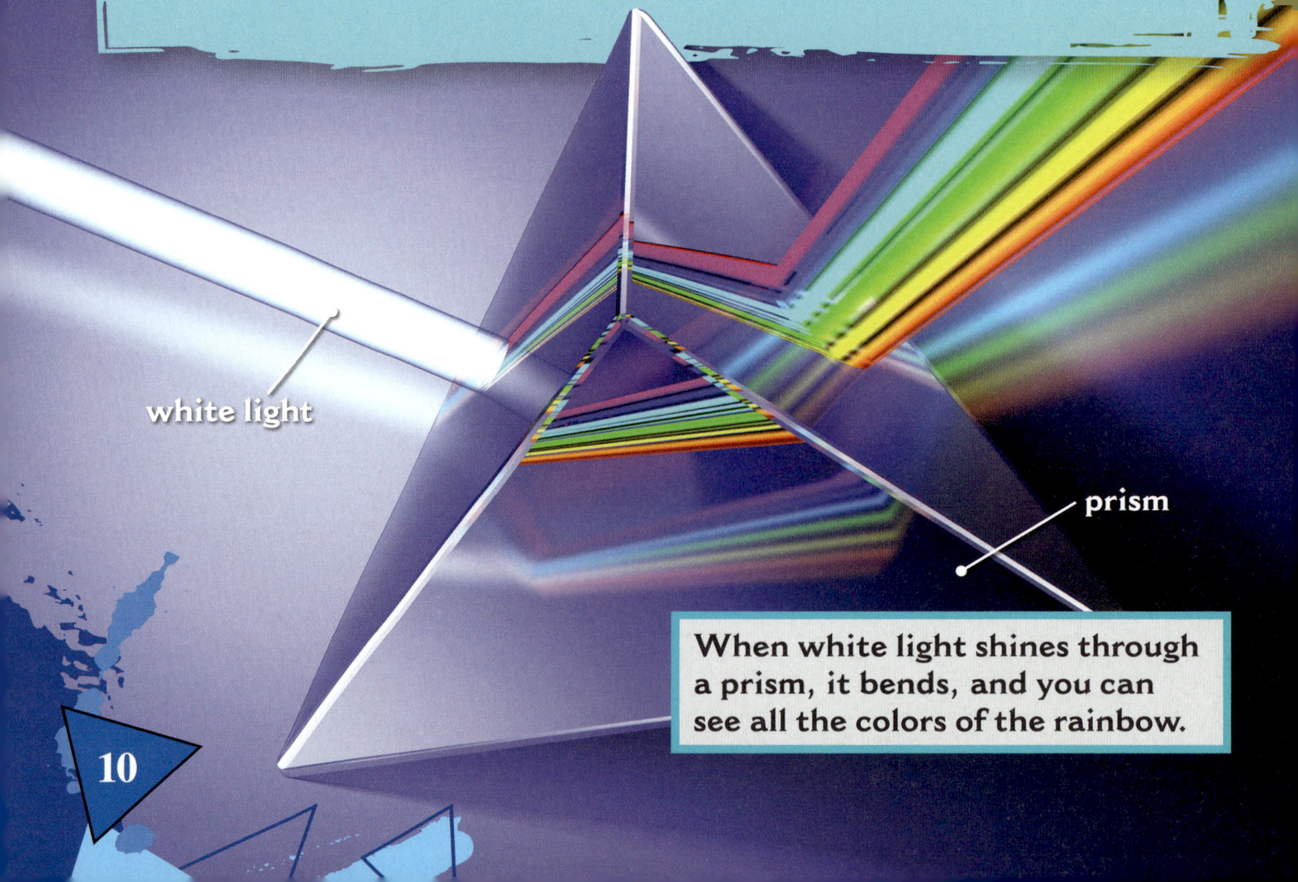

When white light shines through a prism, it bends, and you can see all the colors of the rainbow.

LET'S EXPLORE MATH

Magnus is going camping with his family. Before they leave, he measures the beams of two flashlights. Use the drawings to answer the questions.

Flashlight A

Flashlight B

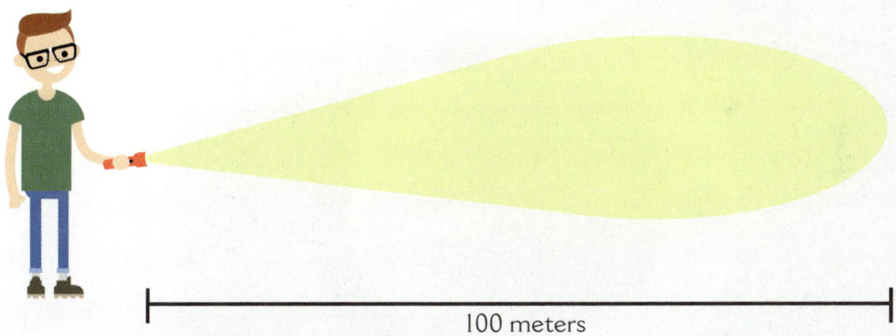

1. Compare the beams using the words *shorter* and *longer*.
2. Why do you think Magnus measured the beams in meters instead of centimeters?
3. Which flashlight do you think Magnus should bring on the camping trip? Why?

Laser light is not white light. Instead, lasers are made up of just one color. Most laser beams appear red. But laser beams can also be yellow, green, or orange. Since a laser has just one color, it also has just one wavelength. That one wave moves at the same speed. The light is focused in a **narrow** beam.

White light sources scatter. When this happens, the light loses some of its strength and brightness. Since laser light does not scatter, it looks brighter.

White light has a beam that scatters.

Laser light has a narrow beam.

All Around Us

People see lasers every day, but they may not know it. Laser lights are used to read prices of items at most stores. They are also used to play DVDs and CDs. Lasers are used in computers, too. If there were no lasers, people's lives would not be the same.

A worker uses a laser to scan in for work.

A cashier uses a laser to read the bar code on a price tag.

LET'S EXPLORE MATH

Trisha works in a warehouse. She uses a bar code scanner with a laser to keep track of boxes. The laser does not have to touch the bar codes on the boxes to read them.

1. Trisha's old scanner could read bar codes from 15 centimeters away. She gets a new scanner that reads bar codes from 43 centimeters away. What is the difference between the two scanning distances?
2. Trisha's manager has a scanner that can read bar codes from 91 centimeters away. How many more centimeters would be needed for Trisha's new scanner to reach the same distance as her manager's scanner?

For Doctors

Lasers can be used in other ways, too. The bright light of a laser cuts like a sharp knife. Doctors use the narrow beams of lasers to work in small spaces. Sometimes, they use lasers on people's eyes. Laser eye surgery helps people see better. Other times, doctors use lasers on skin. Lasers can clean deep under the skin. They can also be used to make scars **fade**.

A doctor prepares to use a laser on a woman's eye.

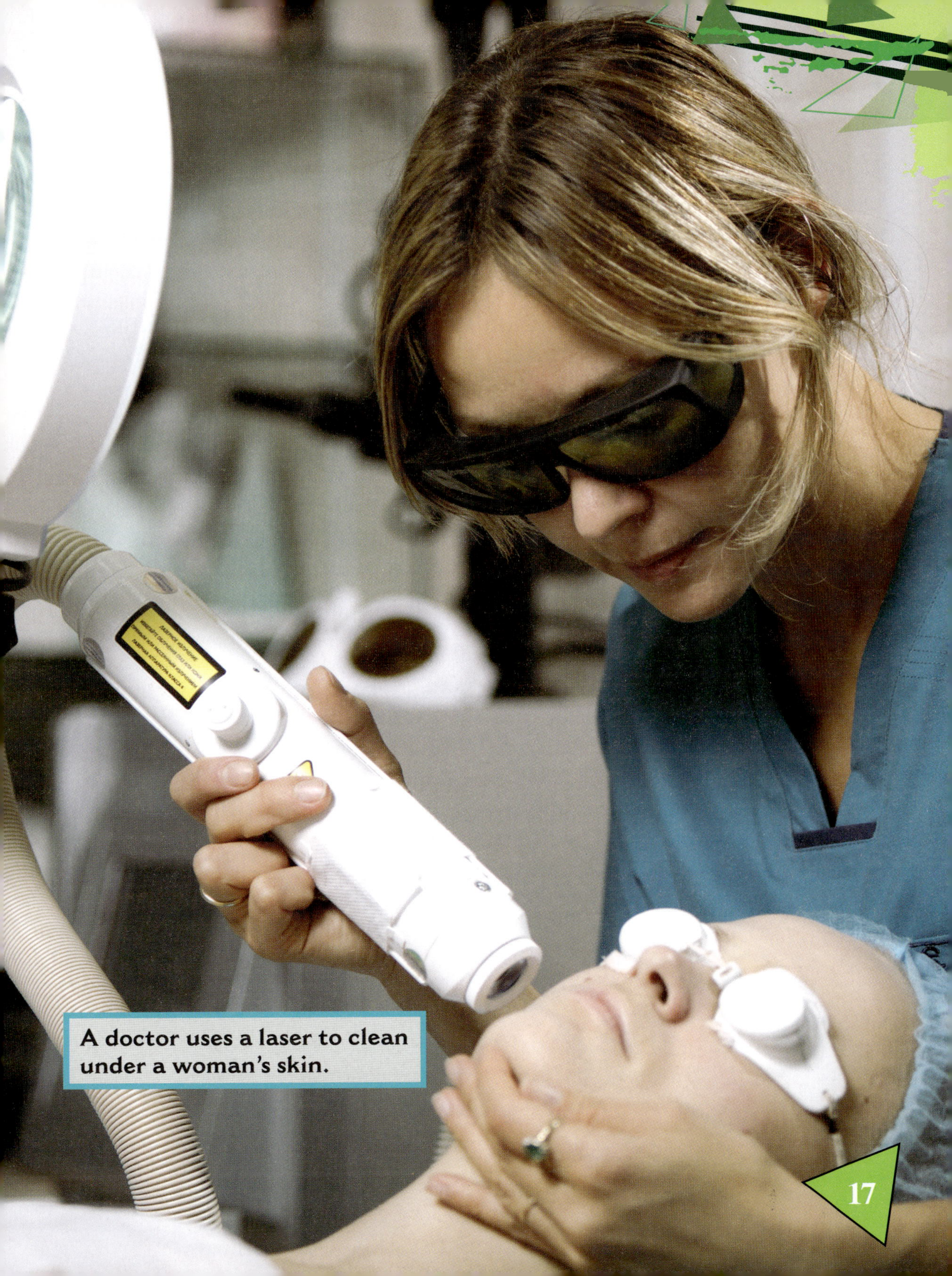

A doctor uses a laser to clean under a woman's skin.

For Museum Workers

Pointing lasers at works of art may seem like a bad idea. But lasers can actually help clean them. Paintings and statues can be cleaned by laser light.

Highly trained people shine laser lights at works of art. The light removes a thin layer from the surface. Dirt, oil, and grease all come off with the strong light. But, people must be careful. Laser lights are so strong that they can take off paint, too!

A man uses a laser to clean the front of a church in France.

A museum worker spent hours carefully restoring a small part of a statue.

For Scientists

Scientists **rely** on lasers to do their jobs. They use them to do things that other tools can't. Many people use tools to cut and drill holes. But tools can become **dull** after a while. Lasers do not.

Scientists also use lasers to measure very long distances. In fact, lasers were used to find the distance to the moon. It would have been impossible to measure this distance with rulers!

A NASA scientist pours sand over a laser.

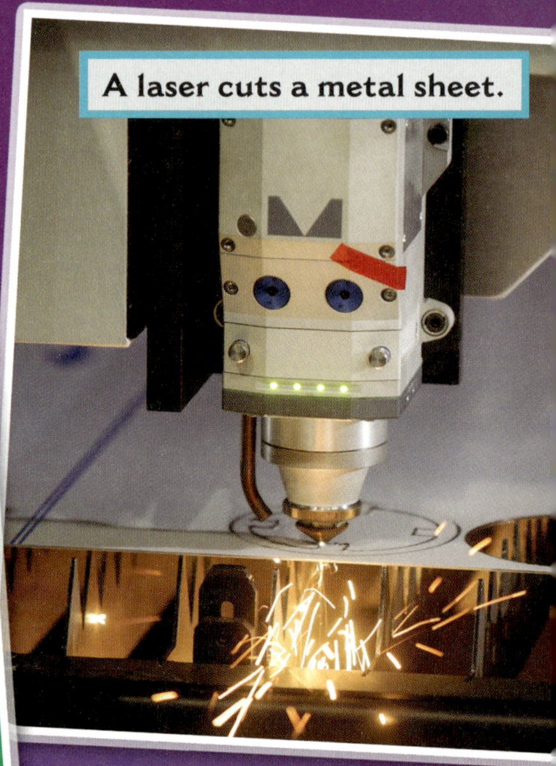

A laser cuts a metal sheet.

NASA scientists shine a laser at a spacecraft to track it as it moves around the moon.

For Builders

Builders use lasers to measure things, too. They measure buildings, floors, rooms, and walls with lasers.

Builders use lasers to make sure buildings are safe and strong. They use them to make sure walls are straight. If walls are not straight, a whole building could fall down!

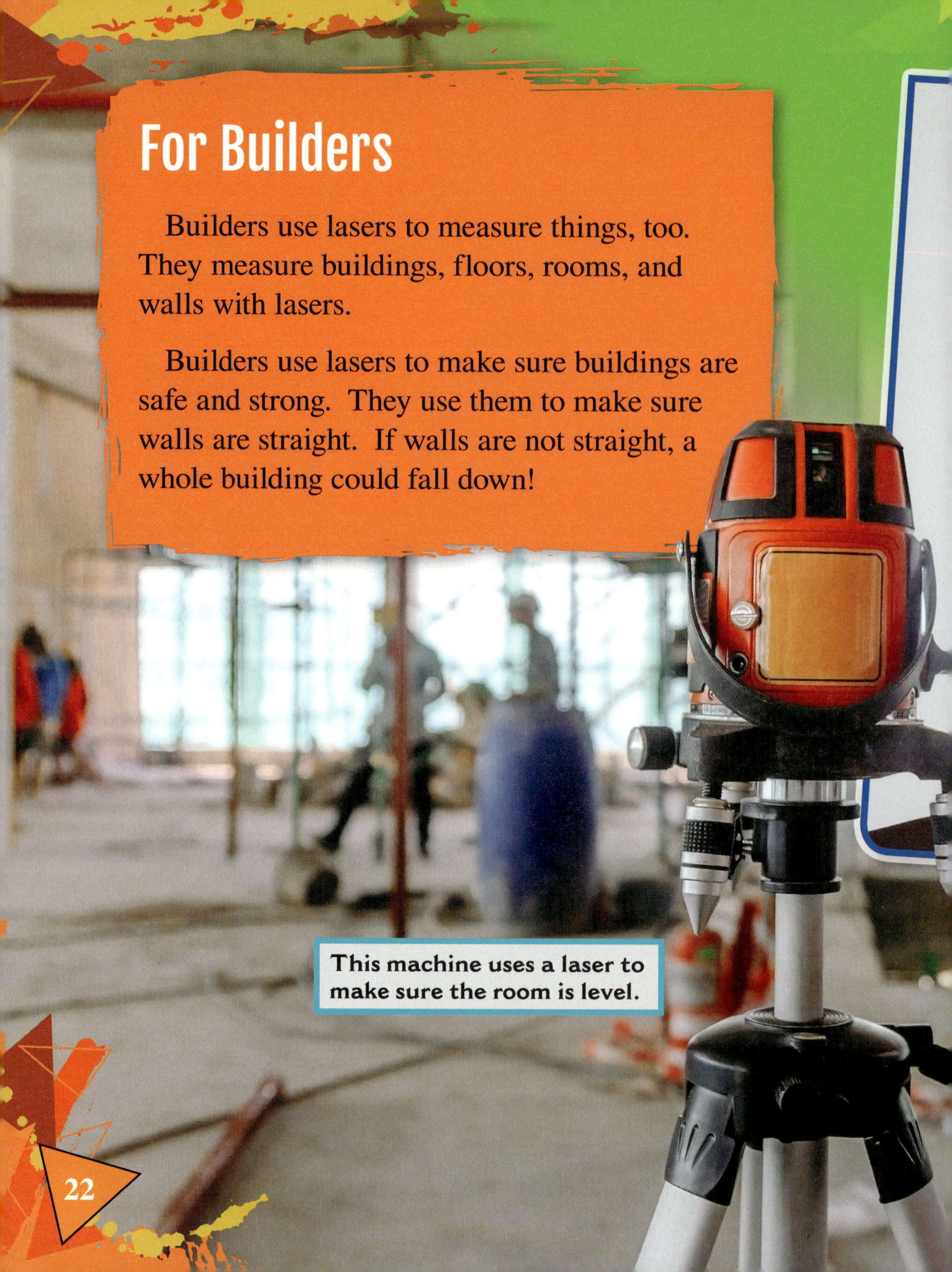

This machine uses a laser to make sure the room is level.

A man shines a laser at an elevator to make sure the doors are even.

LET'S EXPLORE MATH

Imagine that a builder uses a laser to measure the length of two hallways. The first hallway is 72 inches long. The second hallway is 96 inches long. How much longer is the second hallway than the first hallway? Write an equation to solve the problem.

Just for Fun

Lasers can be used in fun ways, too! They are used in light shows. Lasers light up the sky in different colors. Lasers can also make **holograms**, which are three-dimensional (3-D) images. These are used in 3-D movies to make objects look like they are jumping out of the screen. These are all fun uses for lasers!

A laser light show entertains people in Thailand.

People watch a hologram of a man making jewelry.

Lasers of the Future

People use lasers for many things. There will be even more ways to use lasers in the future. Some doctors think lasers can help bones heal faster. Scientists can use lasers to learn more about space. Just imagine all the ways lasers might be used. Maybe you will find a new way to use them!

A NASA scientist uses a laser to learn more about a rock from Mars.

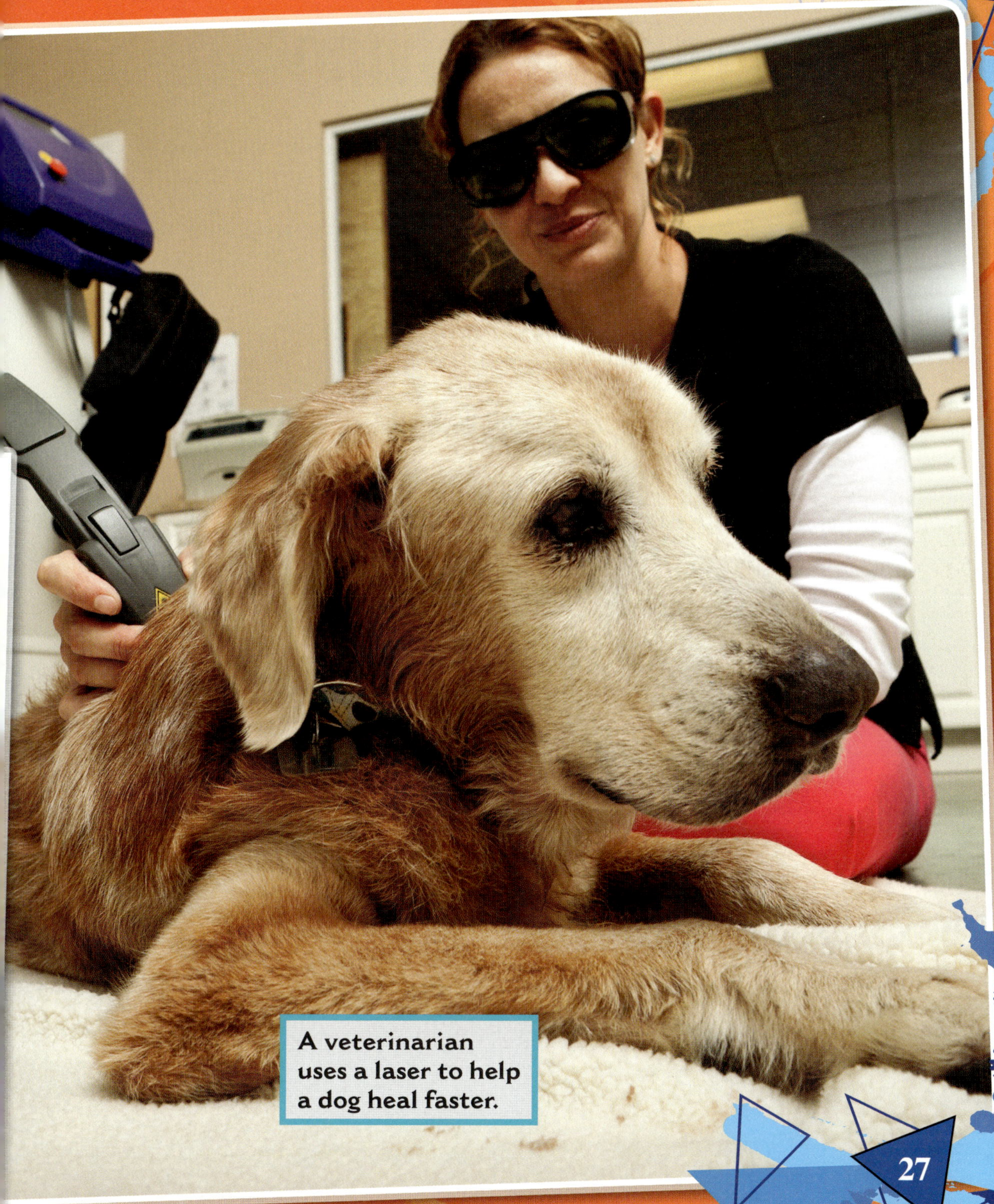

A veterinarian uses a laser to help a dog heal faster.

Problem Solving

Laser light shows are very popular. Some of these shows take place indoors. The lasers are projected onto screens. Answer the questions to learn more about laser light shows.

1. Imagine that a room used for a laser light show is 15 feet tall. Would the room's height in inches be greater than or less than 15? Why?
2. The laser lights are 11 feet above the floor. How many feet taller is the room than the laser lights? Write an equation to solve the problem.
3. Lasers can be projected to the sides of audiences. But, there must be 8 feet of empty space on both sides. How many total feet is this?
4. What is the difference between the empty space on one side of the audience and the laser lights above the floor?
5. In a small room, the laser is 30 feet from the screen. In a big room, the laser is 100 feet from the screen. How many feet farther from the screen is the laser in a big room? Use words, numbers, or pictures to prove your solution.

Glossary

beam—a line of light

dull—not sharp

fade—to become less bright or to disappear slowly

holograms—special pictures that are made by lasers and look three-dimensional (3-D)

narrow—long but not wide

rely—to need someone or something

scatter—to break apart and move in different directions

source—a thing or place from which something else comes

Index

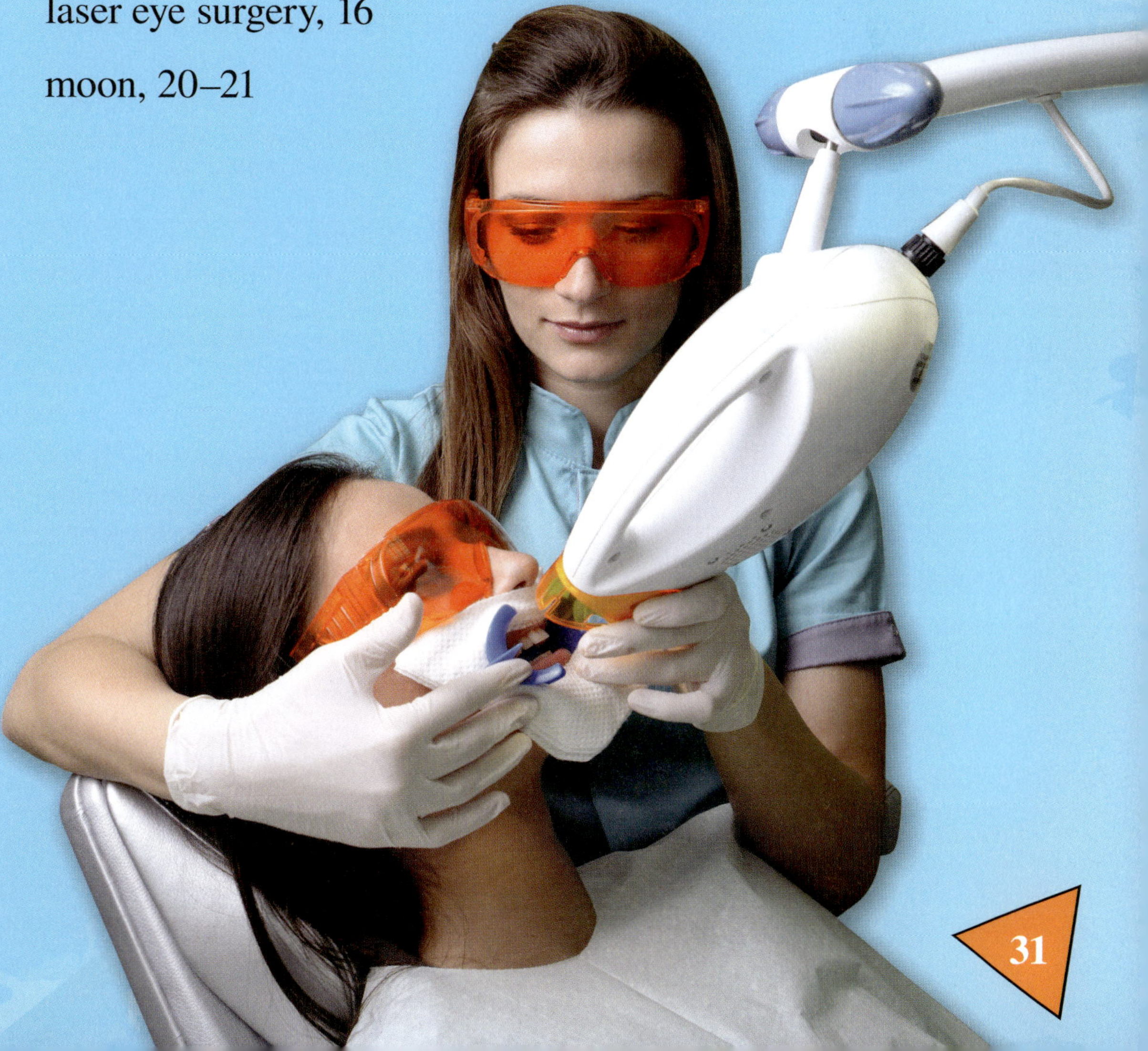

Answer Key

Let's Explore Math

page 11:

1. Answers will vary but may include: Flashlight A's beam distance is 75 m shorter than Flashlight B's; or Flashlight B's beam distance is 75 m longer than Flashlight A's.
2. Answers will vary but may include that meters are a bigger unit of measurement than centimeters, so it would take fewer meters to cover a long distance.
3. Answers will vary. Example: *I think Magnus should bring Flashlight B on his camping trip because the light shines farther than Flashlight A, so he will be able to see farther at night.*

page 15:

1. 28 cm
2. 48 cm

page 23:

24 in. longer; $72 + \underline{24} = 96$ or $96 - 72 = \underline{24}$

Problem Solving

1. The ceiling's height would be greater than 15 in inches because inches are a smaller unit of measurement than feet, so it would take more inches to cover the same distance.
2. 4 ft. taller; $11 + \underline{4} = 15$ or $15 - 11 = \underline{4}$
3. 16 ft.
4. 3 ft.
5. 70 ft. farther; Answers will vary but may include equations, number lines, or skip counting.